Weather A System

James Wilkes was born in Poole, Dorset in 1980. He studied psychology and philosophy and is now working on a PhD about the construction of landscape in the Isle of Purbeck. He also writes art criticism and drama; *Interior Traces*, a radio play about brain imaging technologies, was broadcast in 2009. Previous publications include *Ex Chaos* and *A DeTour* (both Renscombe Press, 2006), and *Reviews* (Burner Veer, 2009). A selection of his work was included in the anthology *Generation Txt* (Penned in the Margins, 2006).

Weather A System

James Wilkes

Penned in the Margins
LONDON

PUBLISHED BY PENNED IN THE MARGINS
53 Arcadia Court, 45 Old Castle Street, London E1 7NY
www.pennedinthemargins.co.uk

All rights reserved
© James Wilkes 2009

The right of James Wilkes to be identified as the author of this work has been asserted by him in accordance with Section 77 of the Copyright, Designs and Patent Act 1988.

This book is in copyright. Subject to statutory exception and to provisions of relevant collective licensing agreements, no reproduction of any part may take place without the written permission of Penned in the Margins.

First published 2009

Printed in Great Britain by the MPG Books Group, Bodmin and King's Lynn

ISBN
0-9553846-9-9
978-0-9553846-9-1

This book is sold subject to the condition that it shall not, by way of trade or otherwise, be lent, re-sold, hired out, or otherwise circulated without the publisher's prior consent in any form of binding or cover other than that in which it is published and without a similar condition including this condition being imposed on the subsequent purchaser.

Acknowledgements

Some of these poems, or versions of them, have previously appeared in *Archive of the Now*, *City State: New London Poetry* (Penned in the Margins, 2009), *Dear Sir*, *Gists & Piths*, *Generation Txt* (Penned in the Margins, 2006), *Great Works*, *Intercapillary Space*, *Leisure Centre*, *Openned*, *Poetcasting*, *Readings*, *Reviews* (Burner Veer, 2009), *Tears in the Fence*, *Veer Off* (Veer Books, 2008), and *Written in Stone* (Artsreach, 2009). Many thanks to the editors of these journals, anthologies and pamphlets. 'London Bridge; or, A Postal for 3 Voices' was originally commissioned for London Word Festival 2008.

~

Thank you to my family, and to all those friends who have collaborated in readings, performances and fabrications: above all Holly Pester and Abi Oborne, Lawrence Bradby and Anna Townley, Sally Davies and Lina Hakim, Ben Borek and Edmund Hardy, Tom Chivers and the Generation Txt poets, Paul Hyland, Artsreach and the Purbeck Footprints group.

Contents

PART ONE: Collected Civil Ephemera

Medical Questionnaire	15
"Clear Sky" Anticyclone: Winter	17
Spring-Summer Collection	18
Carousel Europa	23
Some Theatrical Branches of the Muse's Vine, Which Are Legitimate Topics of Poetry	24
Four Variations on the Same Midwinter	27

PART TWO: The Review Pages

Griet Hannay, *8 Little Curtain Rings*	31
Robert Steinbeck, *The Leaping Pebble*	32
Mary Dundhed, *The Art of the Kilim*	33
Kelly Hobbs, *Inner Glassware*	34
Mahindra Gupta, *Mela Tales*	35
Chris Shaker, *A Dollar and a Half a Day: The Diaries of Isaac Carpenter, Midshapman* (ed.)	36
John Seesman, *Caliphate Pop*	37
Gareth Jenkins, *Handles Brusquely*	38
Celia Fenchurch, 'Experiments in Living Now', and Ella Solinsky, *Eléments Provisoires*	39
Linda Hadley and Edwin Hak, *6 London Fountains*	40
Pieter Peeters, *Delta Blueprints*	41

PART THREE: **Three Purbeck Poems**

    Approaching Cleavel Point   45
    Vanishing Points: Arne   49
    Restless Letters: A Response to Eric Benfield   52

PART FOUR: **Scripts and Transcripts**

    London Bridge; or, A Postal for 3 Voices   61
    Try Enter Doss   62
    Fountain Transcript #3   63
    Fountain Transcript #4   70
    Fountain Transcript #5   72

SOURCES FOR 'THREE PURBECK POEMS'   77

For Sally

Weather A System

PART ONE

Collected Civil Ephemera

...*this weather is the vestibule to something fountaining newly and crucially and yet indiscernibly beyond. Perhaps here we shall be other than the administrators of poverty.*

Lisa Robertson, 'Introduction to the Weather'

MEDICAL QUESTIONNAIRE
STRICTLY CONFIDENTIAL

State if you have suffered from any of the following:

Tuberculosis	NO
A detached voice	YES/NO
Fainting or Migraine	YES/NO
Blood coughing	NO
Proper names	NO
Compulsion to invent devices	YES/NO
Coughing or hoarseness	YES/NO
Sciatica, of long duration	NO
An unholy din	YES/NO
An empire of crime	YES

Is any investigation pending? If so please specify <u>I LOST MY VISION IN A PROVINCIAL STATION AND NOW I OBSERVE IT THROUGH FIELD GLASSES. I AWAIT FURTHER INSTRUCTIONS.</u>

Have you suffered an injury? If so state when and how <u>THE ABUSE OF POWER HAS LITERALLY COST ME AN ARM AND A LEG. THIS WAS MANY YEARS AGO NOW. WITH MY WRITING HAND I STRIKE AND STRIKE OUT.</u>

Are you at present on any form of treatment or medical advice? If so please specify <u>GIVE UP. DON'T GIVE UP. GIVE UP. DON'T GIVE UP. I SELF-MEDICATE BY EATING, SHITTING AND SINGING.</u>

Have you had any specialist advice in the last two years? GET BEHIND VELVET DRAPES. STUMBLE SOFTLY FROM WALL TO WALL. MY GASTROENTEROLOGIST PREDICTED A DIRE SWING TO THE RIGHT BUT I THOUGHT HE WAS STILL JOKING.

Have you lost any time through illness or injury in the past three years? If so, for what and for how long I HAVE LOST EVERYTHING. WHY DO YOU THINK I AM APPLYING FOR THIS JOB? DO YOU THINK IT IS FOR MY HEALTH?

Do you feel in good health? IS ELIMINATIVE MATERIALISM REALLY SUCH A DIFFICULT CONCEPT? LET ME ANSWER THAT, YES. I STRUGGLE TO FOLD DOWN WINDBLOWN MAPS, LET ALONE HUMANITY.

Have any of your relatives suffered from any of the complaints listed above? If so, please state which and the relationship of the person to you IF BY COMPLAINT YOU MEAN COMPLICATION AND BY COMPLICATION YOU MEAN EXISTING THEN ALL OF THEM. START FROM HERE: ADRENAL HORMONES SUCH AS GLUTOCORTICOIDS INCREASE WITH STRESS AND DEPRIVATION AND SUPPRESS NEUROGENESIS IN RATS. NOW RUIN THE TOWN HALL.

How much do you smoke per day? THAT IS A GOOD QUESTION.

"Clear Sky" Anticyclone: Winter

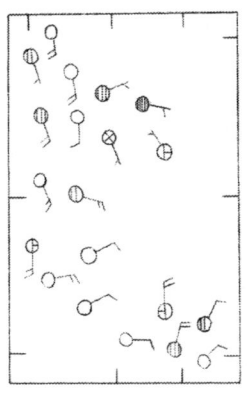

Weather various. Weather up the ocean, where it provides among meteorological ships and data; weather down the aircraft, where it forms also among the flights of intervals and the regular information of a current (and daily) basis. Weather on the main weather report, weather on the synoptic stations. Weather varying into the equipment of functions; weather sending out on the amounts, and being in the frequency of tabulated forecasting; weather being quoted on the headquarters of Dunstable and in full hours. Weather in the times and pages of front back observations, being taken by the hour of intermediate April; weather in the air and afternoon of some pressure of the primary *millibars*, down in his nine mercury barometers; weather continuously obtaining the scales and attachments of the changing upper column on height. Aerological mercury on the atmosphere being replaced over the barograph into a following reading of sea level, with weather all instrumental, as if it supported a rate, and could be measured in exact rises.

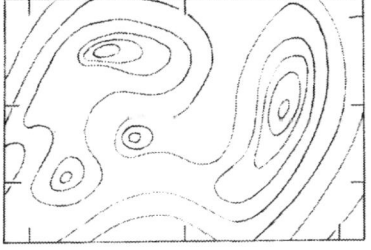

Spring-Summer Collection

This is ethereal cannonade. This season's acoustics: snare pops, crunch and yodelling. Correspondents shift uncomfortably and thumb their paperbacks until: autonomous movement, first model out walking fast and radical. For inspiration, think the legs, tucked and extended, in old horse paintings, so her canter swings sufficiently the hem. No coincidence that Technotronic's *Pump up the Jam* reverberates the glittered plywood. Released in 1989: Solidarność legalised, the Wall in ruins, the Velvet Revolution. Surely this Belgian new beat classic thus picks out choreography to plead a European pose contra neo-lib hegemony? – Yes but what about her clothes?

> iridescent
> buttons
>
> pleats (still
> bounces
> with
> resid-
> ual
> swing)
>
> navy &
> ochre trim
>
> a nice
> hat

Correspondents embellish as she turns, and her double emerges from the wings. Significant details: the vestigially protective aspect of the collar; the soft flare and gather of material at the spine; how light can be coddled to do this; the mauve gloves; the paisley. Chiasmus as they pass, the swaying balance of retreating night, advanced severity in pin-stripe. Couture tilts unpredictably against the bias, a surface happy under strip lights or a cavernous pigeon sky. The covering is slashed, reveals an undercover – orange, louche, and redolent of cooking. Calm, she stops,

> bearing all
> the lines
> of business
>
> the return
> of figures
> ruptures
>
> soft power
> of allure
> haunted

for an audience. Her footfalls crash with sudden loss of faith, the weathered end of wealth her economic turndowns at the heel. Transparent baubles bursting in her tress, and veined like estuary surfaces her jacket's sea-glass cincture plays opaque; she saunters off. Makes room for tartan whimsy, repurposed panels stiffly cut and held with cleats and ribboning. Nothing says informal economy like tarpaulin, it's almost like the plastic weave itself is aching to enfold around her as a bag:

> upholstery
> staples
>
> glint and
> hold her

a short
-term
contract
with cerise
dungarees

as the DJ hides the seams and house's corridors extend their vanishing colonially through this. And OMG, a shawl is flicked around her shoulders like they're knocked off Fendi bag and run before the carabinieri crack some skulls, enamelled lemon lacquer on her thinly ridged and stacked-up heels, she wavers and she vanishes before our eyes. Silence, silenzio, and the next look marries the sea, which is a kind of people, an irregular unpleated stance. What supple canes maintain her new and ample blue as field of crumpled zones around the working legs, whilst at the apex of disturbed habiliment parades a precious manikin. Awkward to hold, a delightful clutch,

slipping
shearing

violet torn
white flecks

tectonic
round the

knees, elbows
worn to a

collage of
movement

and display
and topped

with a
jesus handbag

She executes a volta: collective gasp, her back is bare and tattooed with a pensive St. Jerome, big and red and leonine in Ray-Bans and outrageous headgear. She offers up a beatific pose, balancing the pedals expertly on kitsch and gas. We need some more like her. Now listen: I know a fabric where the onion is raw like silk – but shop talk is as short as breath. A petrol hairpiece keeping pace with scintillating sugar-cane cement hits town, a single hairpinned length unrolling,

of chance
ikebana, like

Wolfgang
Tillmans

composed
the jumpsuit

from tea-water
window light

& grains
of Super 8

that smear the stage. It's all going turmeric until the techies intervene, slap the filters on above and turn the whole thing coral. It must be for the sailor's cap, or possibly the pea-green coat which hangs like calving ice – and falls as the DJ mashes *Tainted Love* with a rare translation of Raymond Carver into French. A mellow sonority of rum and shag: *soudain, je trouve un nouveau chemin à la cataracte*, though correspondents note the laser-cut and porous bangles effervescing from ankles up to thighs: well.

A cropped
fawn
ziggurat

& palettes
there
to be
broken,

fuchsia
malachite

& bolts of
camel

would say that wouldn't it? But thanks to penicillin, skirts are floatier now we're not afraid of catching death and forced to fend it off with horsehair, cummerbunds and oil. The merest updraft billows out the carefree voiles, the kicked-up plumes and bronze and open canopies. The scent unwraps like complex chestnut chandeliers. So ciao to caution, ciao to solitude, from here you balance like you mean it, a one-shouldered cut against a dazzling azalea. Sophisticated *and* populist: with detailing so asymmetric, how can it go wrong?

Carousel Europa

Heading south   vers le sud
The wind blows hustle and
The sky turns
Vendredi   j'ai vu tué   Winter

After the night
Il vento fa il suo giro
Great silence
Lève-toi et marche   Citizen

Some Theatrical Branches of the Muse's Vine, Which Are Legitimate Topics of Poetry

1. Bike Couriers

A bike couriers' soirée might happen in an abandoned multi-storey with fluorescent tube lights propped in corners, cans of iced beer sold from a wheelbarrow and a choice of hard trance or the music of falling concrete. Post-industrial minimalism may be démodé but they do it with flair.

Also bike couriers are interesting because they shuttle desirable items through smog and danger. Such as contracts, deeds of sale, blackmail demands, blood samples, gigs of unrefined data, fashion accessories, and high-res satellite shots of factories in Guangdong.

These piratical nomads service capitalism on the cheap risking bodily injury in the forced spaces between membranes. Power needs differential (see watermills, synapses etc.) and if two membranes touch all information disastrously finds its level and is called a merger.

So bike couriers are like butchers or meat packers, whose jobs are also quite dangerous and who are trusted despite appearances. Not hypocrites, they confront complicity in keeping the boundaries cruel and functional. But for a poet what bike couriers have over butchers is a sense of style.

Heavy red twill ripped off at the knee. Bike oil, sweat and headphones, bleach and clippers, ornament the brain case. The heavy hardened links the waist. The tweaked-out racers, oilskin bags and radio static blur. Who would not want to glamorise these fast people?

2. Fireworks

Their saltpetre trajectories are split at the root. One traces the destruction of all good surfaces, the horrific ruin of epithelia. It pollutes the other, yes and spices it, the depth and artifice the flat sky gets lent.

They are liked by small children though not by pets. And indeed, children don't neglect to write poems about them. This tendency creeps in with adulthood and is a mistake. Up, up up! Tris! Tris! Bang!

They sketch a ghostly commons from incandescent specks. It is our chemical weather, susceptible to drift, ornate mixture of earth and breath. Even for a private celebration, they are sent up over the wall.

Solitary and emulsified by rain, or packed in so the cordite pricks each nostril. No-one trusts them, the claim to pure expenditure and nothing back, the way they compel a crowd to crane upwards.

3. Palletised Freight Distribution

When the engine shuddered fitfully at fleas, a dreaming stop light, then we liked to sing, o muse, an economical sparrow ditty didn't we? Something plastic so we could freight it around, over choice junctions in our hollow bodies.

I noticed that palletised distribution liked the radio, stippling far ends of the warehouse with bonhomie and pop. Like that time we were all in one room and sick of its symmetrical contents, we slopped a bucket of reflected din and affect up the walls and down towards the forklift.

And the poor softwood dogsbody splintered in the corner. When music doesn't reach you then you've earned your rest. We'll crowbar you apart whilst drivetime bubbles from your lips and fabricate a lovely picket fence or line.

At least that's what I used to think. Since then I've realised that comparing intermodal units to Paul Klee or anything else is great dishonesty. The networks that furnish us with cadmium orange aquarelle, with lypsyl, watchstraps, condoms and polenta, are military surplus. So what? The lights about to change. Our loaders are idling at Rotterdam docksides, sparking their plentiful cigarettes. We're all distorted by the leverage. Drive on.

Four Variations on the Same Midwinter

The gold cover and
the world breathing birth to zero.
The weather bleached of haunt.
It's now love, to decline.

~

Breath witness
of hare's haunt, and sheep's.
Fire now. Light me.
Don't dim beside day.

~

Light's lower rip to curtain
so I stood breathing the weather of hare and sheep.
If ever it's still, inquisitive and bright.

~

Through eve, so
birth the barrow the fields.
Un-flowered on blether
need roused fingers and rise
brimming.

PART TWO

The Review Pages

Griet Hannay, *8 Little Curtain Rings* (Strasbourg: Ed. de Canard, 1989), 16pp.

A psychotropic longhouse becomes the locus for this eminent rehash. Its structure is cantilevered thus, so the balcony's long shadow bunches at my throat. The entrance is a revolving door, a kind of promiscuous lock. Inside many young Belgians bodypop their continental ennui.

This becomes a poetry of lampposts, dogwalkers, poplars, theodolites, bus stops, municipal statues and radio masts. All the lonely civil spikes. Here is everything to do with comfort, acoustics, light and shade. I was magnificently bored.

Robert Steinbeck, *The Leaping Pebble: a Philosophical Novel*, ed. and foreword by James Lewes, Gertrude Felix and Sabrina Harms (Edinburgh: Stott Books, 2002), 198pp.

Speculative biomedical ethics meets dancehall reverie in this elegant folio reprint of the hard-to-find private press original (1908). Editorial cuts by Lewes et al. are largely faithful to the author's intent, unlike Kendal's bowdlerising excisions of 1934 (though see Selene Camphor, 'Kendal, Steinbeck et le problème de proprioception' in *Études baltiques* 65 for an alternative view). Relocating the scene of the ambiguous sexual encounter from Behlersee (Schleswig-Holstein) to Battersea (Wandsworth) is an interesting move, though it does make the appearance of the famous black stork a bit anomalous.

For anyone with even the slightest interest in whether the neural correlates of consciousness might be understood via a bedsheet tied to broomhandles on which coloured images flurry, settle, detach like film of ashes, this is a must. Otherwise wait for the stage adaptation. If chatroom gossip is correct, this will be set in Thessaloniki circa 2030, and opens with Ludwig (Robert Redford) attempting to fence DNA stolen from a medieval saint's fingerbone.

Mary Dundhed, *The Art of the Kilim* **(Paris: Overboard Editions, 1994), 128pp.**

The Friend laughed and pointed at the kilim, the technologised surface, he exclaimed. Later I used a wi-fi heart and unknotted this as best I could.

The blueprint for a kilim is improvised live, in the maker's cob and breezeblock heart, he said. He smiled for effect and popped a roasted chickpea with his teeth.

The Friend prefers a glass of water, he thinks this is the happiest of drinks. I cleverly switched his for gin, and when he was tipsy I slipped my fingers up his sleeve and stole his expensive heart.

I was lying in a burned-out basement as the Friend interrogated me harshly. Streaming tears, I asked why I could never see his face. He extinguished the heart and approached.

We wandered moodily along the beach. Between the greedy cows and beach huts of the Soviet, between hypodermics, twisted fishing nets, the bloated carcasses of dogs. This too is a prayer rug, the Friend announced. Playfully I slapped his heart.

Kelly Hobbs, *Inner Glassware* (Exeter: Mintleaf Press, 1996), 4pp.

The author is a longtime resident, this gentle tearing as of tissue down the page. A loving object liltingly, the greased paper refuses. Hatched and hatching, a spring song in pondwater mortality.[1] More or less open, "refusing the birdsong intravenously" (Frangipani: 43).

The second poem opens and doesn't stop, unfolds to the skies like a good bit of architecture.[2] Unmachined as a broken chainsaw buoyed upwards by burnings of woodsap, hazel, birchbark, charcoal, withies, gumboots, campion. Then it's over.

A longer pages, no more rural but still with a sense of name. Illustrated delicately, with red pink and ragged of political tension. The darkened tenderloin. Petrol chard and gumboots, again.[3] More fen shoe than feng shui, more thin dingo than fandango. Six out of ten.

---

[1] The information is hiding in the margins, trying to disappear (being made to disappear).

[2] As in, the blurred print run-off in the deepest rivers.

[3] See Jeremiah Randal, *Towards a Modern Understanding of Bovinity* (Bristol: Fanfare, 1927).

Mahindra Gupta, *Mela Tales* (Mumbai: Samizdat Publications, 2006), 182 pp.

Mahindra Gupta, staff writer on the *Bombay Samachar*, is sent to cover the Maha Kumbh Mela. 60 million people camping together induces in the narrator first nausea, then vomiting, shortness of breath, flashing lights, and a series of psychotic fits or visions. Here are our favourites:

3, "Mahabharata spacecraft like silver cigarillos in the dusty air." Done archiving the silent wastes of space, Garuda descends to earth. His flightpath darkens half the city and the clap of tungsten wings over Chowpatty Beach collapses the eardrums of a bhel puri seller named Mahindra Gupta. He has to explain this to his wife. It is essentially a slapstick farce.

8, "Had an elephant smelt it he would have slept from night to night." A man finds himself stuck in an intertextual mugging of the *1001 Nights*. The following substitutions may be made: the love-struck merchant for balding car mechanic Mahindra Gupta. The three eunuchs for his drunk nightwatchman pal. The date tree for a roadside dhaba on the Delhi-Agra road. The beloved Kút al-Kulúb for the contaminated drum of engine oil and the dread Caliph for Gupta's sinister employer, the improbably-named American investor Claude Claus. It is a satirical detective story, more or less.

#14, "She sat at the window, drawing on a cigarette. He could see her mouth and fingers in its irregular glow." Gupta is invited to a friend's wedding in Arkhangelsk. Afterwards the bride comes to his room and sits at the window smoking endlessly. He makes a half-hearted and unsuccessful attempt to seduce her, then lies in bed and watches her in the darkness. It is a kind of post-Soviet rom-com.

A Dollar and a Half a Day: The Diaries of Isaac Carpenter, Midshipman, ed. by Chris Shaker (Rochester, NY: Perceval Press, 1994), 120pp.

Guano verticals elaborate a coast. Fog-phantoms, a pickled beef vibrato, the rigging. So a simple nib trembles cutters and here's a soft basin, a basalt uprising of melted birds (in the sparse notes, a melancholy ecosystem that *don't need a tar's presence*.) A nebulous and not overly-caulked dawn approaches, verbatim and musical, proceeds in sailcloth parallels, and ridged networks of mollymawk. Isaac Carpenter's best on weights and measures, rhumb lines, salt meat, set and drift. His grandson's pebbledash intricate across the masthead. But where's the folks gone? Their voices crack the vitreous, the tiling, best on the terrible weather. Still they should be more.

John Seesman, *Caliphate Pop* (Manchester: Doves and Demons, 2005), 36pp.

Secret graphic underside stops the opening, a spread of flaming lines. This made me think of 5 new licks, 1) If *a* stands at intersection of ley lines x and y and forms a bleated origami shape, will the Kings X Channel Tunnel borehole fling an upsurge of celestial waste? Several rational minds disappeared into the sewers or else the Metro chanting a poem about a 30-foot carp. It swam the Grand Union for pleasure.

If you ever find yourself in a room with John Seesman, ask him to tell you the story of how he lost his thumb. Go on, ask him. 2) Is there ever a good way to tell your lover you'd rather fuck a leather cosh? 3) English cathedral Gothic is revived in the brushed aluminium carts and upraised brooms of agents employed to sweep the frequencies. Paolozzi's Newton was strapped in his chair and smoked welders spectacles for everyone to see. All in all, an intriguing debut from the author of *Celtic Horse Mysteries for your Cat*.

Gareth Jenkins, *Handles Brusquely* (Rhyl: Long Tenpin Books, 2003), 48pp.

Nothing like Eminem. Nothing like my yucca plant refusing to die. Nothing like a small town in the Pyrenees in Lent. Nothing like a painful occupation. Nothing like Kandinsky's *Composition IV*. Nothing like Chick Corea. Nothing like the ocular shimmer of my beloved undressed. Nothing like the Krebs Cycle. Nothing like swag. Nothing like a swagger-stick oompah noise and crowds. Nothing like an infinite generative grammar, or any of that. Nothing like Pat Barker. Nothing like Dutch portraiture. Nothing like fish rising to take the fly in spring.

Nothing like a small town refusing to die. Nothing like my painful composition in spring. Nothing like an undressed Krebs. Nothing like Kandinsky's ocular shimmer, or the Chick Cycle. Nothing like an infinite generative oompah noise and swag. Nothing like a Lent Barker refusing to plant. Nothing like the flies rising from occupation. Nothing like a swagger-stick shimmer taking the crowds, Pat. Nothing like my beloved Pyrenees fish. Nothing like a portraiture swagged by Corea's pain, or any of that. Nothing like any Dutch yucca. Nothing like Eminem.

Celia Fenchurch, 'Experiments in Living Now' in *George Scorsese: New Works*, ed. by Julian Boschild (London: Passport Gallery, 2005), 144pp.

Ella Solinsky, *Eléments Provisoires* ([Paris?]: [n. pub], 1977), 40pp.

Dear Blog, hello. In urban cammo trousers I am nearly elfin, blotchy, Palmeresque. Two books balance in my cargo pouches. One advances in baroque sweeps, the other its undoing, cuts away. Hello pigeons. Will you be my archivists? Hello plane trees. Will you be my audience? All shake their heads with masterful disdain.

O self-indulgent blogosphere, hello. The upstairs flat is drilling too much coffee through my brain. Increasingly I fear (*je crains*) people (*purple*). Kinky and inchoate. If they were voles I'd feel remorse, breaking their spines, but they're just books. Two of them balance in my seeping cortex. My interests: abandoned vehicles, affordable warmth, airports, ants, beach huts, beaches, beauty treatment licences, bees, benefit fraud, cemeteries and crematoria, chimney heights, complaints, compliments, cooling towers, council tax and how it is spent.

Increasingly I ache for (*désire*) completeness (*complexity*). It gets out of control, in the suburbs, in early summer. Demonstrations and parades, dentists, drainage, emergency planning, ferries, floral displays, fly-posting, fridge-freezer removal. Going into hospital, great trees, gritting, harassment and violence, hedges (high), hedges (overgrown), highway flooding, home from hospital, how to do business.

I'm tired now and crave dried figs and water. Lampposts, libraries, licences, litter bins, lost dogs, major incidents. Mapping. Meals on wheels. Micro-chipping, opticians, roundabout sponsorship, street furniture, street naming, traffic data, wasps. And all around the moon hangs up its gentle running spikes to dry.

Linda Hadley and Edwin Hak, *6 London Fountains* (Canterbury: Panda Press, 2008), 8pp.

One ragged sheet they complicate down, a small hand-inked dribbler, of slit and fold and press within the pages. 13 spumante pencils, the central higher than the rest.

The "rational fountain", bisected by the shadows of financial courts, turns water to a fabric draped unwrinkled over marble slabs. But a wobble turns a ravel, and it seams.

The dampened husk and scaffold of a civic flow: the blocked stone fountain gathers surplus, of material, of rainspots, in the park.

Pieter Peeters, *Delta Blueprints,* **trans. by Claude Claus (New York: Panoctagon Books, 1998), 90pp.**

If two homing pigeons descending in a rotary blur got tangled this translation would release one and retain the other for its records.

If Le Corbusier and La Baker had done it in a Flanders motel this translation would be midwife to their mewling offspring.

If you were looking for a place to live this translation would offer delightful and useless suggestions.

If the *coloratura* of words could somehow be divorced from their *ligaments* this translation would be there with a crowbar.

Sometimes there's an after-effect, green on black, or is it pink on blue? The shapes are boxy concertinas anyway, expanding wheezily through streetlight.

A sand bar, a love hotel, a prison hulk, a nylon arcade.

PART THREE

Three Purbeck Poems

Approaching Cleavel Point

1. Once I halted on the wide grassy plateau over Ower, stopped at the Private sign. Now I can say: I passed that sign, crossed that cattle grid, went down that track. I have been trying to read signs of occupation off the land. The new ones are not always obvious. The old ones buried, broken, scuffed.

2. *Marine transgressions*, meaning silting and erosion went to work here. Medieval furrows interrupt Romano-British. *Islands of survival*. The poetry of archaeology is a palette of description, just as exact and just as broad as it needs to be.

3. The first was in a boiler suit and said, I wouldn't bother, I'd just go down there. He was raking something down from the hedgerow, or perhaps he was cutting it. What was he doing? Working. Sorry to interrupt you. The second *was* down there and though at first I hesitated, his evasion suggested no more right to be there than us. It's right here – when cornered at the water's edge – it's right here just go round the corner, and his excitable lurcher pawed my father with red tinsel in its collar. *Hedged in with a surer pale than wood*. All on a Boxing Day trespass. The gate was open and the pumping station hummed.

4. A technical language, a thing of beauty, a palette to work in, to grind and puddle.

    Animal bone, marine molluscs, burnt bone, shale;
    Ill-defined gullies and scoops;

'Burnt' soils varying from dark grey through light-brown to bright;
Marine molluscs, undulated lenses;
Mottled muddy clay, raw white clay;
Marine shell, briquetage, crushed charcoal, flint.

5. Left of the door, an earplug dispenser. Do not enter pump room when red indicator is illuminated. Check status of fire and gas panel. This site has been de-classified to a non-hazardous location. Ex Certified Equipment is not essential for safe operation. Right, a fire alarm weathers to pink.

6. *Artefacts perform active metaphorical work in the world in a manner that words cannot. They have their own form of communicative agency. I felt it gently between my fingers, but found much earth mixed in.*

7. Brent geese, afloat in the offing, covertly synchronous. Impossible to detect the moment they swing, but now all weakly magnetised another way. Perhaps a net, of edging relations between neighbours, and Purbeck edges into harbour, back and forth through abutments, mudbank, channel, reedbank, marsh, puddle, piling, inlet, flintbank, creek, shingle, deep, lake.

8. *Trespasses of vert and venison*
   that Henry Smedemore, John Stoppe, John Cole junior,
   and others whose names are given
   entered the King's warren in the night
   of Sunday next before the feast of St. Valentine
   with a net and a dog
   to take the King's deer
   and the said Henry and John with their net and dog
   are now in the castle of Corfe

9. The archaeologist's descriptions are care embodied. There is a particular language that objects speak, an oblique, obdurate song. Notate, translate, publish.

   This is salvage poetry, and the jumbled mess I've made of numbered pits and kilns *occupational debris*, more like looting. The legality of this occupation is in question. When is it not? I've disturbed the context, covered the paw-prints tracking back and forth.

10. *When the tide ebbs*
    it has the appearance of a vast swamp. Nothing
    under the idea of landscape can be more
    disagreeable.
    In some parts, when the tide is full,
    and you can get a few
    trees into the view, you have a tolerable Dutch
    ~~landscape~~
    > human encounter
    > territorial thrashing
    > production & waste
    > rusting trough
    > mineral prospect
    > clayed fingernail

11. Karen shows me a few sherds from when she worked on the dig. All black burnished ware, BB1, the local stuff, thick, dark, unglazed, each fragment dense to the hand, rubbed to a polish when leather-hard.

The silent conversations of things
        fill the air
throwing human shapes in sharp relief.

Here was formerly a pottery.

12. The sun slips into the fabric of the reeds through listed fragments of imported Arrentine ware.

Slip, red, mirror bright; extremely smooth;
Slip, thin and washy, very variable through dull red-brown to orange-
                                                           brown;
Slip, thick dark red-brown, smooth;
Slip, very smooth; scorched.

Fabric, pale buff to light 'dirty' yellow;
Fabric, pale-pink, with plentiful mica;
Fabric, pale; scorched;
Fabric, pale, somewhat coarse; very slightly burnt.

Vanishing Points: Arne

1. It was already late when my friend started talking about the ethics of law. *Juris-diction – speaking law – can only be ethical when no-one records it. Because if it's recorded, it can be cited, used to condemn people*, she said. I slipped this in my notebook, sly-jointed stenographer, crab-handed: the ethics of transience. Our talk drifted sideways.

   The night drains away and is gone. The night bus, swinging its articulated bulk down the Whitechapel road, drains of fluorescence and is gone. The towers and offices of the city, strung networks of light and power, fade into a mist, and are gone. Hours away down main and branch lines, dawn in the Arne reedbeds, a slow greying increase of light.

   Here is Arne the heathland parish, as the social historian reads it, its slow decay, the piecemeal buying up of copyholdings by Poole merchants, the speculation, the overreaching that ruined families, creeping back to Wareham as household servants and small traders, *decayed yeomanry*.

2. Where's ethics when subsistence farming means just that, nothing to tide over one bad harvest or one unexpected death? More pressing for now are the ethics of writing the past, of resuscitation.

3. *Acid podsols with a humus-packed top horizon and often an unmanageable iron pan two or three feet from the surface*, writes Barbara Kerr. Standing on that strip of unexpected beach where the heath suddenly falls into the sea, Long and Round islands

to my back, the banked earth in front: black tendril roots of ling grope the air.

> Now the mosses and the grass
> open with sure fingers
> the flower of his skull.

Stepping out east on the track from Arne church and the old school house, the concave sweep of the fields on the left, early enclosed, only bit of good soil around. *It is doubtful if open arable farming was ever practised on the East Dorset heath soils* – Kerr in my ear again. Enclosed but not amalgamated – that came later. And the Poor House at Jackhams, 1801, the quiring of curlew in the long low tides.

> Move more marginal. In space and then in time:
> Upper horizon: flat, luminous grey, with hints of rain over
> > Hamworthy.
> Boot level: chalk lumps, wintering over, the frost to break
> > them apart, ineffective.
> Spade level: acid black humus, leaching the yield.
> Lower horizon: sandy, ashen grey.
> Rock bottom: ironstone, iron stream, the brown water
> > trickling over sand.

Furze and sour soil and heath. Burnbake, lime and back-break. A little rye, a little oats. *Fat hen, corn marigold and spurrey.* A townwards drift. Bracken.

4. Enough of that. The Poole merchant families have always had their eye on this. Prestige and politics. Is it elegy you're after? How about: Farm Labourer, Farm Carter, Carter's Boy, Pupil Teacher, Brickmaker Labourer, Brickmaker, Scholar…

composed of strata
    or layers of turf
    played out within a single body of space

...Housekeeper, Housemaid, House Servant, Former House Servant, Proprietor of Houses, Road Labourer, General Labourer, Dressmaker, Former Laundress...

socially and mentally demarcated
    an endeavour to shut out the encroaching sand

...Clay Labourer, Boatman, Naval Pensioner, Ship Carpenter, Cowboy, Carpenter Journeyman, Farmer of 200 Acres, Servant, Farmer of 100 Acres...

what is permissible and what is not
almost plaited together

...Gamekeeper, Invalid, Clay Digger, Clay Miner, Clay Cutter, Schoolmistress...

an abode, a place, a secret place
deeply indented and broken

Restless Letters: A Response to Eric Benfield

1. There are words. Words on words, a bare plateau swept by glare and shadow. A habitation, a handful of books. Crossed by paths of willed opinion, pungent anecdote and memory, that lead across it, down inside it, word linked to word, joining and spreading. Towards what?

   You have been dead for more than fifty years. Perhaps the first I should wish is your hope fulfilled, an *absolute end in complete blackness*, the *comforting friendliness* of annihilation after death. In which case there is no 'you'; this is a letter that will never reach its address, a letter with no possible completion, stamped with what you called the stone worker's curse and due to be restless on the earth, a fellow traveller –

   > I mean for the words, the remainder
   > drift of scars
   >   from a ghost outline
   > fallen from an absent shape
   > soundless chiselling of
   >
   > heaped leavings, & the years-long trickle
   >
   > brush of warm fingers
   > finds it calcified, strains to crack it
   >
   > the fragments indifferent
   > in libraries or stone yards.
   >
   > *Stone is impersonal and*
   > *above the fretful froth*
   > *which is called Life*

a phrase turned awkwardly but true – *out of winding* – the stone always hanging over life's head. The great weight of it, *dying to come*, underpicked. Massive, annihilating, beyond your or anyone's strength to deflect. The arm you described as well-shaped, a quarrying sculpting restless arm: always under a precarious block.

2. The occulted strata of certain images. A man is working several hundred yards from the foot of a shaft and knows that *every inch of the way is darker than the night*; to meet even his wife, his thoughts *have first to travel consciously along that black way*. A dark lane and a deep separation of thought; this is not only about someone winning their livelihood in the hardest of ways.

A man is testifying at a religious meeting, and inclining his body to indicate the narrow lane and working alone by the light of a single candle; *now and again bursting into song for the sheer bitter glory of God*. Certain details have a strange power to annihilate distance and time. They hit a note that rings out through ruined stone huts and worked-out quarrs and re-configures the present.

3. Or, this is not enough. Not enough to have been taken for a few brief minutes underground. To have seen by candlelight a few walls, joints, picked-up legs, the clay squeezing out – *like soap* – between blocks of downs-vein, curling gently upwards over two hundred years since the last heavy-hobbed boot climbed out.

Those particular worlds, of loneliness without fear for you, or of hunger blood and visions of devouring fire for James Corben a hundred years earlier, of walking across the dark and densely-knitted fields, climbing down into the earth's bowels, crawling along the dark lane and finally sparking a flint near the damp rock-face, are gone. The vertiginous blossoming of time down there, mingled with steaming breath, is over. The fields have unravelled their charcoal wool, and it is full of holes.

> It's not enough.
> Because I can climb out whilst it's still light.
> Leave, drive away
> the spacing of life shrunk to a petrol blur.
>
> Maybe I only imagine I'm the one moving:
> Purbeck as a stony whale, carrying its dead
> away under the stars but
> relative displacement, let's say that much.
> So what can come from such
> asymmetry, of positions and trajectories?
> Why write a letter?

4. Because I come after, wanting to understand. Because you wrote with the passion of exile, and respect enough to yarn and gossip and blast your fellows. Because you were sometimes so profoundly wrong. Because the words are a common inheritance, to be claimed for the living, for now. A working definition of respect. I hope, I believe, that an inheritance is *the reaffirmation of a debt, but a critical, selective and filtering reaffirmation*. That it's possible to untwist, to choose between.

– hymning the active body:
– the folding of this
– proud and stubborn,
– and wound with
– a debt: for adding to
– to repay: take up the work
        running, carrying, lifting, labouring
        with domination
        an independent spirit
        a coldly vicious
        the edifice of Purbeck
        always unfinished
                for purpose or sheer excess –
                or possession –
                stitched brazenly through feudal fabric –
                misogyny –
                leaky bundle sprawling on –
                of bringing forth a place –

At the foot of the cliffs of Durlston Bay, amongst the rocks beneath the landslip, someone has pulled bleached trees into a protective hurdle for a fire and mattress, trunks with roots like horns. Below them a ship's hawser has rolled and tangled itself proud of the cliff's wreckage, polypropylene turquoise against pale stone. It is braided from a loose handful of thick coils, each coil made from hundreds of strings twisted together, over and over. In places the outermost fibres have been rubbed to a mass of tassels.

Many stories, intertwined, conflicting; many versions wound together. Sometimes there are spaces between them and with a twist they can be persuaded apart.

5. No fixed essence; no essence. A dry stone wall running along the flank of a valley, redundant besides three strands of barbed wire stretched between wooden posts. Crooked fingers of ivy, growing through the sockets and joints of the stones, gently distorting their lie. The brush of warm fingers, over dry cut grass, over a weathering memorial. Thistle stumps I scraped away with my boot. The rough patina, dust on my fingers, a small gesture of honouring.

Part Four

Scripts and Transcripts

The following pieces are sourced from radios, conversations and other overheard sounds. They are intended as prompts for performance, so if reading them in your own voice gets tedious, borrow some others and do it as a group. Buses or post office queues will serve as auditoria.

The fountain transcripts faithfully reconstitute conversations between Lawrence Bradby, Sally Davies, Lina Hakim and James Wilkes that took place as they drifted around London looking for fountains one Saturday in 2009.

London Bridge; or, A Postal for 3 Voices

Voice 1: City AM, City AM, do you get City
Voice 2: Vine leaves. Hot but not spicy hot
Voice 3: Fizzy hot?
Voice 1: Yeah! Came up in blotches all over my face and neck and
Voice 3: Well my job's not in jeopardy
Voice 2: She asked me to dance. You unnastan?
Voice 1: Lethal. That cherry juice
Voice 2: But I will arrange for a plumber
Voice 3: Absolutely fucking lethal once you get a stain
Voice 1: And if you get any flak speak to um
Voice 3: Dot gov dot uk or you can call
Voice 2: To take the doors off or just do it out of hours
Voice 1: Some people are impressed by that

  (Pause)

Voice 3: I, er, work for the Croydon Advertiser
Voice 2: Only in dreams can I feel this way
Voice 3: But I love trawling through everyone else's rubbish
Voice 2: Crackers, cheese, I love crackers
Voice 1: Well why not. A Superclub in the heart of Loughborough with first 30 ladies
Voice 2: By any means possible. Have you got any serviettes?
Voice 3: Everything for a girl like you
Voice 2: Souf London's finest, on tap
Voice 1: Tell us the brief history, please, of
Voice 3: The UK this Saturday the 25th of November

  (Repeat with Variations)

Try Enter Doss

After César Vallejo

Never seen, enters no event never calories as
Rum, but wrap her rack chest.

Serpent beneath her, you tell Miss Cock's hero
And jeer her father Tin Pan alley-o!

Key in. Come o loss, heal us. Pair or not.
Key in (comma) lock quaver-knee maths-knee maim us.
Key in (comma) hell's just a medico.

Milk cow or he has
Azaleas Irene – hey! Sugar and catch harder
Hell's firmament goes grin goes by her
Hell so limp a vase of lily all berate her lost cash co.
All maths free to

Remedy all cooks to roué. Eeeeee! Hisss!
Tear no auto's grill, move ill the cess
Cake or I hassle the player.

Air! Air! Hello!
Seal Mania Hits Girl, or may or
No dig or nada.

He has to lammy his plume or
Conquer a scribble, poor Baltimore's a trencher.

Try enter his kestrel on his tress, he lent us tree entrance he trains
                                        callow for us.

Fountain transcript # 3 – 03.37

Lawrence: It's. It's a fairly quiet revolution.

James: We've. We've found, we've found our public fountain, we've found the – the civic flow that we've been looking for today, here in Clerkenwell, in Spa Gardens no less, I mean this is historically —

[Camera shutter]

James: Appropriate. [Pause] Is it not?

Lawrence: Wh – why?

James: We're in Spa Gardens and I presume it [inaudible]

Lawrence: Ah yeah.

James: Kind of... spa.

Lawrence: Yeah.

Lina: [Laughs]

James: [Laughs] From the word 'spa' in the word, in the name 'Spa Gardens'.

Lawrence: Yeah. Yeah. And the fountain itself seems to be modelled as if it's – a bit of a building site. With the corrugated iron.

James: Yeah. Yeah. We've got this. Well I mean corrugated iron is, is, vernacular, isn't it, really. [Pause] It's a vernacular material.

Lina: [Inaudible]

James: Sheds.

Lawrence: Yeah, although actually we haven't seen much of it today have we?

James: Well I'd say it's rural vernacular. You know? Instead of like, instead of – cottages made out of – wattle and daub – it's corrugated iron. These days.

[Siren in distance continues under]

Lawrence: No I think of it more as a fifties sort of...

James: Really?

Lawrence: Material.

James: Well was that the high point of civic uh —

Lawrence: [Laughs]

Lina: [Laughs]

James: You know is it a reference to that, to that. That post-war settlement, that's been undercut. I mean we are after all outside the back end of a restaurant which... I think potentially might have been the place, where Tony Blair and [inaudible]

Lawrence: It may well have been.

Sally: Very well!

James: I mean we've got this whole kind of like, strangely rigged kind of exhaust happening here.

[Siren quite loud here]

Lawrence: Oh yeah that's made that one poplar tree go all black.

Sally: [Laughs]

James: Yeah.

Lawrence: That's taking all the hot air out, isn't it.

James: It is.

Lawrence: From the uh –

James: From the kitchens.

Lawrence: From the realpolitik deals being done inside.

James: Yeah, hell's kitchen.

Lawrence: Mmm [sniffs]

Sally: [Laughs]

James: Yeah. Well. I'm quite excited about it.

Lawrence: I'm quite. I would have been more excited for... The potential, to see people gathering round here and drinking from this.

James: Yeah.

Lawrence: And squirting each other.

James: Yeah.

Lawrence: That's what, that's the kind of...

Sally: But the weather's not really – yeah.

Lawrence: Social interaction... That one might see.

James: Yeah. [Inaudible] This is the kind of quiet, I mean this is not, this is not exuberant, this is just...

Lina: Well maybe they'll play.

James: We've got some people playing football...

Lawrence: And also importantly there's no... Benefactor's name on it.

James: No this is [inaudible]

Lawrence: [Inaudible] just for drinking, it's not for memorialising.

James: Yeah. Yeah. But I like the way it does encourage a particular stance to be taken.

Sally: Mmm.

Lawrence: Although we haven't worked it out because...

Sally: You would be drinking upside down.

Lawrence: Are you - are you really expected to drink like that?

James: Well I don't know.

Lina: Well I think the hands held... [inaudible]

Sally: Wasn't the idea that you spit in that way?

Lina: [Laughs]

Lawrence: Spit that way?

Sally: Well, you know, so you're not, you know. [Pause] You know like normally with a drinking fountain or whatever.

James: You have to gargle?

Sally: Yeah maybe.

Lina: Maybe it's teamwork. One person goes on top and then the other person has to...

Sally: Yeah, yeah yeah.

Lina: Hang from them.

Sally: [Laughs] Maybe it's —

Lawrence: It's not obvious how...

Sally: Maybe it's so you can actually lean in.

Lawrence: Oh yeah.

Sally: Is that the idea? Or you lean from one side.

Lina: What if you're really tall though?

Sally: [Laughs]

Lawrence: So maybe you, you drink and then your friend is standing up here...

Lina: [Laughs]

James: Just in case!

Lawrence: Saying go on, go on —

Sally: Go on, drink.

Lina: [Laughs]

Lawrence: [Inaudible] their head in like —

Lina: Ow!

Sally: I think – you'll actually find that's probably like a health and safety thing because like if a child was to run...

Lawrence: Uh-huh, ok.

James: He'd get stopped on the soft concrete.

Lawrence: [Laughs]

Sally: [Laughs] they get stopped [inaudible] concrete. So I think it's to stop people.

Lawrence: Oh ok.

Sally: Maybe. Like it's that sort of... Demarcation of the space around it. But equally it could be [inaudible]

Lawrence: I, I think, I think you're right actually, I agree. But it does make it look like you're supposed to —

Sally: Climb up.

Lawrence: Like a, like a mounting block.

Sally: Mmm.

James: Ok.

Recording ends

Fountain transcript #4 – 01.30

[A single drop of water falling every 0.4 secs (approx.) from a laundry outlet pipe onto the plastic casing of a burglar alarm below. Continues under]

Lina: Very elaborate [?]

Sally: It's so quiet down this [inaudible]

Lina: [Inaudible] [laughs]

Sally: [Inaudible]

James: This is lovely look at this.

Lina: [Inaudible]

Sally: [Laughs]

Lawrence: [Inaudible] Is that what you meant?

James: Yeah.

Lina: [Inaudible] the wall.

Sally: Yeah yeah, it's got little um.

James: And you've got kind of algae on this side and moss on that side.

Lawrence: Look at the beautiful new – wall here.

James: Yeah.

Lawrence: It will be rotting.

Lina: But this thing will attack that one if it grows enough that will be cool.

James: Yeah.

Lina: [Inaudible]

Sally: Oh but that's just cladding that's just brick cladding. I think.

Lawrence: Yeah.

Sally: [Inaudible] you can see there's like [inaudible]

James: [Inaudible] It is actually spray. You've got. We are standing in the spray [inaudible]

Lawrence: I wouldn't call it a fountain I'd call it a waterfall.

Sally: [Laughs]

James: A water feature maybe.

Lawrence: A water feature.

Lina: It's a bit like those. You know these – games, where the –

Recording ends

Fountain Transcript # 5 – 02.23

[Hiss of fountains. Assorted voices in background]

James: Trafalgar Square.

Lina: [Inaudible]

James: Twenty to seven.

Sally: [Laughs]

Lawrence: Friday the 13th.

James: Saturday the 14th.

Lina: [Laughs]

[Voices in background]

Lina: The plugs[?]

James: Groups of people. No-one swimming.

[General laughter]

James: Um, exuberant water.

Lawrence: Sal! No, don't you'll get really cold!

James: People —

Sally [Laughs]

Lawrence: Oh let me hold your bag anyway Sal.

Sally: [Laughs]

James: People clearing up after some kind of – [inaudible]

[Voices in background]

James: Celebration... Ah, I heard a, I heard a little chuckle of someone being scared of being pushed in there.

[Pause. Voices talking]

Lina: Maybe we should just go look at it to see what happens.

James: [Laughs] Ah. Now look there's a whole group of people in yellow caps coming through.

Lina: Ahh.

Sally: [Inaudible] lots of people taking photos, and they, you know being frustrated by the fact that, with the flash it doesn't quite work,

James: Aye.

Sally: You don't get the same effect. Very beautiful, when you look at the steps.

James: Yes.

Lawrence: Occasionally the, a little gust of wind takes a lot —

Sally: Yeah.

Lawrence: A load of spray out of this fountain and drifts it over towards all those, um, arc lights —

James: Well um I —

Lawrence: It's quite exciting as well.

James: Because actually when the, when the wind came our way we were engulfed in a sort of little... cloud. And then perhaps you know that, there's there's hope there, for um. You were talking about this, the fountain being controlled and channelled like the public... protest that's, that's permitted here but um, you know...

Sally: Constrained...

James: Yeah. The, the wind of change might be a-coming. I mean it's not —

Lawrence: Ride that metaphor Jamie, keep it going.

James: Well you know we've just seen these posters here Storm the Banks, um —

Lawrence: Yeah.

James: These some kind of vaguely anarchistic, certainly quite angry —

Lina: Emergency.

James: Yeah, yeah.

Lawrence: Capitalism in Crisis.

James: Yeah. Ah here we go look, the wind is changing direction and actually we're getting... [Pause]

Sally: A bit damp!

James: We're getting dampened by the mist of public...

Sally: Civil —

Lina: [Laughs]

James: Yeah civil —

Sally: Like glory.

James: I don't know what to call it.

Lawrence: Civil drizzle.

James: Civil drizzle. This is a civil – we're in a civil drizzle. And it's quite nice.

Recording ends.

Sources for 'Three Purbeck Poems'

These poems are the result of walks and research undertaken as part of the Purbeck Footprints project, and incorporate material from the following sources.

Barbara Bender (2002), 'Contested Landscapes: Medieval to Present Day', in *The Material Culture Reader*, ed. by Victor Buchli

Eric Benfield (1948), *Purbeck Shop: A Stoneworker's Story of Stone*

Eric Benfield (1942), *Southern English*

James Corben (1996), *A Langton Quarryman's Apprentice, 1826-1837: James Corben's Autobiography*, ed. by R.J. Saville

Jacques Derrida (1994), *Specters of Marx*, trans. by Peggy Kamuf

John Hutchins (1861), *The History and Antiquities of the County of Dorset*, third edition, ed. by William Shipp and James Whitworth Hodson

Barbara Kerr (1968), *Bound to the Soil: A Social History of Dorset, 1750-1918*

Sophie von La Roche (1933), *Sophie in London, 1786: Being the Diary of Sophie von La Roche*, trans. by C. Williams

Federico García Lorca (1935), *Llanto por Ignacio Sánchez Mejías*

Nigel Sunter and Peter J. Woodward (1987), *Romano-British Industries in Purbeck*

Christopher Tilley (2002), 'Metaphor, Materiality and Interpretation', in *The Material Culture Reader*, ed. by Victor Buchli